# Give me half an hour

## 23 Topical Short-Short-ETAs

## Klasse 9

Autoren:
Dr. Peter Fenn
Jürgen Kienzler
Renate Kienzler
Gottfried Kumpf
Gerlinde Kumpf
Eric Orton

Beratung:
Dr. Peter John Dines
Phil Grayston, Leeds

Illustrationen:
Yvonne Brix
GUS
Rosanna Pradella

Photos:
Jürgen Kienzler
Gottfried Kumpf

Best Nr. 7404 ISBN 3-928156-34-9

## THE BIRTH OF AUSTRALIA

In the 18th century poverty and unemployment were common in Britain, and for many stealing food was the only way to survive. Thieves were sent to prison for long periods of time. Jails in England were dirty and unhealthy places. Men, women and children were all crowded together. When the prisons got overcrowded, thieves were hanged, or transported to prison colonies in America. After America had become independent, however, these colonies were lost.

So Britain had to find other territories overseas where prisoners could be sent. The solution was Australia. Captain James Cook had discovered the east coast of this enormous continent in 1769, and had claimed it for Britain. Nearly 20 years later ships full of prisoners and prison guards arrived in Australia. The first prison settlement was established by Captain Arthur Phillip near Botany Bay (where Cook had landed). The area was named New South Wales. It was many years before free settlers began to arrive in the first Australian colony. That is why most modern Australians say that their forefathers were "criminals". Today Australians celebrate the birth of their country on January 26th, "Australia Day", the date of Captain Phillip's arrival in 1788.

### A. Comprehension

***Read the text and answer the questions in complete sentences.***

1. Why were so many people sent to prison?
2. Why weren't the prisoners sent to America any more?
3. Why shouldn't Australians proudly say, "My forefathers arrived with one of the first ships in Australia"?

### B. Language

***Write a complete sentence to explain the meaning of the following words.***

1. prisoner
2. colony

***Write down the words in the text for***

3. persons who steal things
4. a group of simple houses where some people live

***Complete the sentences by using the opposites of the words in bold print.***

5. **birth** A war usually means ... for a lot of people.
6. **dirty** A restaurant kitchen must be very ... .

***Replace the verbs in bold print by words or expressions which mean more or less the same.***

7. A lot of people were put in **jail.**
8. The British wanted to find new **territories** overseas.

***Use the words in brackets to make new words and write them down.***

9. (settlers) The English .... in America and other continents.
10. (solution) The problem was easily ....

**Tenses**

***Write down the correct verb forms.***

11. (to discover) After Cook ... Australia, (to claim) he ... it for Britain.
12. (to celebrate) Every Australian ... "Australia Day".

## C. Translation

***Translate the following text into German.***

When the prisons got overcrowded, thieves were hanged, or transported to prison colonies in America. After America had become independent, however, these colonies were lost. So Britain had to find other territories overseas where prisoners could be sent.

## D. Guided writing

### 1. Asking questions

1. ... ?
*Peter:* My forefathers came to Australia in 1899.
2. ... ?
*Peter:* No, this wasn't my grandfather. That was my great-grandfather.
3. ... ?
*Peter:* I think he came from Birmingham in Britain.
4. ... ?
*Peter:* No, he wasn't a prisoner.
5. ... ?
*Peter:* Yes, he brought his wife from England.
6. ... ?
*Peter:* No, he has never been back to England.

### 2. Writing a report

***Here are some old pages of a diary. Can you write this man's biography (Part 1) in about 80 words?***

| | |
|---|---|
| January 6, 1774 | James Spencer born in London |
| July 24, 1790 | no school, no job, hungry |
| December 24, 1791 | very cold, nothing to eat, steals overcoat and potatoes |
| February 21, 1792 | James was caught stealing food |
| March 2, 1792 | judge sends James to Australian jail |
| March 15, 1795 | James free again, starts working on a farm |
| September 1, 1801 | James has his own farm |
| August 3, 1805 | James has enough to eat, lots of sheep |
| May 10, 1807 | James marries Sally Fields |

## FLYING DOCTORS IN AUSTRALIA

This was Jim Newhart's unlucky day. As usual he was working on his father's sheep station about 300 miles away from the little town of Cobar in New South Wales in Australia. But today he stepped into a hole that a rabbit had dug and broke his left leg. He crawled back to his jeep and drove to the sheep station. His leg hurt terribly and he almost fainted when his father at last helped him out of the jeep. Unfortunately the nearest hospital was hundreds of miles away.

So Jim's father had to call the flying doctor of the district on the two-way radio. A doctor advised Jim's father on how to take care of the patient. Then he asked about a suitable landing site near the sheep station and typical landmarks so he would be able to find it. The doctor took off in a helicopter and was at Jim's bed about two hours later.

The helicopter took him to the district hospital where he got medical treatment at last. Thanks to the Flying Doctor Service Jim soon got well again, but years ago he could well have died far away from a doctor. Each of the flying doctors has a district to take care of which is about as large as France. They often have to get to their patients through dangerous sand storms or heavy rain in the rainy season of the year.

### A. Comprehension

*Read the text and answer the questions in complete sentences.*

1. Why did Jim break his leg?
2. Whom did Jim's father call for help?
3. What sort of weather is most dangerous for the flying doctors?

### B. Language

*Write a complete sentence to explain the meaning of the following words.*

1. sheep station
2. landing site

*Write down the words in the text for*

3. a kind of aircraft that doesn't need a runway
4. a person who is ill in hospital or needs a doctor's help

*Complete the sentences by using the opposites of the words in brackets.*

5. (densely) Australia is ... populated.
6. (easier) Flying a helicopter is ... than flying a plane.

**Tenses**
*Write down the correct verb forms.*

7. (to break) After Jim ... his leg, he drove back to his parents.
8. (to break) ... you ever ... a leg?
9. (to get) How ... you usually ... to hospital?

*Look at the words in brackets and write down the corresponding nouns.*

10. (to advise) Jim's father needed the doctor's ... .
11. (to fly) The ... to hospital took a long time.

**If-clauses**

***Complete the following sentences.***

12. If you break a leg in Germany, the ambulance (to take) … you to hospital.
13. If the helicopter hadn't taken Jim to hospital, he could (to die) … .
14. If I (to have) … a lot of money, I would visit Australia.

## C. Translation

***Translate the following text into German.***

Thanks to the Flying Doctor Service a lot of people are rescued each year. Years ago they could well have died far away from a doctor. Each of the flying doctors has a district of the size of France to take care of.

## D. Guided writing

**Letter writing**

***Jim Newhart writes a letter from hospital. He tells his parents about***

- how he flew to hospital (problems with the helicopter?)
- the time it took to get there (2 1/2 hours)
- terrible pains all the time
- operation (at once)
- pains not so bad now
- three more weeks in hospital
- doctors and nurses very nice
- visit from parents possible?
- perhaps with neighbour's plane

***Write about 80 words.***

Billy's favourite school subjects are games and music. He likes them because he is good at them. And he is good at them because his hobbies are playing football and playing the guitar. He's been fond of playing musical instruments since he was seven. First it was the piano, then the trumpet, and at the age of 11 he started with the guitar. He still plays the piano sometimes, but he gave the trumpet up because he wanted to concentrate on the guitar. He is a member of a local band called "Dynamite". They perform every Saturday night in discos and youth clubs.

Billy's Saturday is very busy. In the morning he plays football for his school first team. Mr. Benson, the games teacher, talked to Billy about becoming the star-player in the school football team. Billy can't decide on a career. Should he become a footballer, or a pop singer?

## A. Comprehension

***Read the text and answer the questions in complete sentences.***

1. What are Billy's favourite subjects?
2. When did he start to play the guitar?
3. What does Billy do on Saturdays?

## B. Language

***Write a complete sentence to explain the meaning of the following words.***

1. a disco
2. a band

***Replace the verbs in bold print by words or expressions which mean more or less the same.***

3. They **perform** every Saturday night in discos.
4. Billy is the **star**-player.

*Find the correct prepositions.*

5. Billy is good ... playing the guitar.
6. He is also fond ... playing football.
7. He is interested ... the music lessons at school.
8. The games teacher talked ... him ... his career as a footballer.

## C. Translation

*Translate the following text into German.*

Billy has been playing musical instruments since he was seven. First it was the piano, then the trumpet, and at the age of 11 he started with the guitar. He still plays the piano sometimes, but he gave the trumpet up because he wanted to concentrate on the guitar.

## D. Guided writing

### 1. Asking questions

*Billy has just produced his first record. You are a reporter. Ask Billy about his musical career.*

1. Ask him when he started with music.
2. Ask him about his instruments.
3. Ask him about other hobbies.
4. Ask him how much money he makes through his hobbies.

### 2. What about you?

*Write a report of about 80 words.*

What do you do in your free time?
Would you like to work in your free time?
Say why.

## PROBLEM LETTER

A letter to Marion Williams, a journalist who writes the "Problem Page" of a local newspaper.

*Dear Marion,*

*My daughter, who is now 16, used to be a quiet, homely girl. She never went out, and didn't have many friends. We used to do everything together. [I've been divorced from my husband for six years]. But in the last six months she has completely changed. She goes out every evening and comes home late. She won't tell me who her friends are, or what she does with them. I've tried to talk to her, but she just won't tell me her secrets. I'm very worried. I think she may be seeing boys or taking drugs. What can I do?*

*Yours sincerely,*

*Mrs Elizabeth Bolton*

### A. Comprehension

***Read the text and answer the questions in complete sentences.***

1. Why is Mrs Bolton worried in the evenings?
2. Why doesn't Mrs Bolton talk about her problems with her husband?
3. What does Mrs Bolton's daughter do in the evenings?

### B. Language

***Write a complete sentence to explain the meaning of the following words.***

1. a secret
2. quiet
3. worried

***Write down the words in the text for***

4. Someone who usually stays at home and doesn't go out very often.
5. A person who writes articles for magazines or newspapers.
6. A man who is married to a woman.

***Complete the sentences by using the opposites of the words in bold print.***

7. Mrs Brown has been **married** for five years now.
8. We do everything **on our own**.

## C. Translation

***Translate the following text into German.***

Dear Mrs Bolton,

Thank you for your letter about your daughter. I fully understand your problem. May I suggest that you spend your next holiday together with your daughter? Try to share as many experiences as possible. So you will win your daughter's trust and confidence again. Then she will probably tell you more about her life and friends.

Yours,
Marion Williams

## D. Guided writing

### 1. What do you think?

***Say whether you agree or disagree with the following statements and why.***

***Choose only two of the following statements.***

1. Mothers and daughters should always do everything together.
2. Parents should always know where their children are.
3. Children should always talk about their problems with their parents.
4. Children should spend the evenings with their parents.

### 2. Letter writing

***Now please write a letter to the worried mother. Write about 80 words.***

Tell her

- that children get older and more independent
- to talk with her daughter about her own problems
- to go out with her daughter
- to share her daughter's interests
- to talk with her daughter's teachers

## EXCHANGE STUDENTS

When Sandra saw the name "Oxford" on the sign she was very excited. This was the place where she and twenty other students from her school were going to stay for the next three weeks. All of them were asking themselves the same questions: What would their new friends and their English families be like? Would they feel homesick after a while? What would English schools be like? Would they have to speak English all the time?

Sandra looked curiously at the small houses which looked very different from the houses at home. Then they saw a large group of people standing in front of a school building. They had arrived at last. Many of them were waving. Suddenly Sandra saw Sophia, her exchange student, who had spent three weeks with her in Germany the year before. She was sure that her stay in England would be a success.

### A. Comprehension

***Read the text and answer the questions in complete sentences.***

1. What did Sandra feel when she arrived in Oxford?
2. How many students from Germany were going to stay there?
3. Why did Sandra look curiously at the houses she saw?

### B. Language

***Write a complete sentence to explain the meaning of the following words.***

1. a sign
2. homesick

***Replace the words in bold print by words or expression which mean more or less the same.***

3. People were standing **in front of** the school building.
4. She was certain that her stay would be a **success**.

***Write down the correct tense of the following verbs in brackets.***

5. Sandra (to be) ... very happy when she (to see) ... Sophia.
6. Sophia (to be) ... to Germany the year before.
7. They (to be) ... sure that Sandra's stay (to be) ... a great success.

### C. Translation

***Translate the following text into German.***

Sandra stayed at Sophia's house for three weeks. She was very happy there because everybody was very kind to her. She liked the large English breakfast with orange juice, tea, bacon and eggs, toast and marmalade very much. Every day she joined Sophia and they spent the whole day at school together.

## D. Guided writing

### 1. Asking questions

***The English students wanted to know everything about Sandra. So they asked her a lot of questions. You ask their questions now. Ask about***

1. Sandra's age
2. her home town
3. her hobbies

### 2. Letter writing

***You also want to spend three weeks in England. You have just received the address of your exchange student. Write to him / her about yourself. The following ideas might help you:***

- name
- age
- school you go to
- favourite subjects
- free time / hobbies

***Start the letter and end the letter with suitable expressions. Write about 80 words.***

# WHAT THE GERMAN STUDENTS THOUGHT ABOUT ENGLISH SCHOOLS

After their stay in England the German students were asked what they thought was different about the two countries.

Some of the Germans thought that wearing a school uniform was very strange because they themselves could wear whatever they liked.

Above all, the German students felt that the school day was very long. Pupils left their homes at about 8 o'clock in the morning and didn't return until 5 p.m. There was not much time left for hobbies or sports. After the pupils had had their evening meal and done their homework most of them stayed at home indoors. They often watched TV or listened to records and then they went to bed. If they went out during the week they mostly went to a youth club, a leisure centre or visited friends.

The German visitors found that Saturday night is the big night in the week when most of the young people go out. They spend the evening at discos, go to the cinema to watch a good film or have a party at a friend's house.

## A. Comprehension

***Read the text and answer the questions in complete sentences.***

1. What did some of the Germans think about the wearing of school uniforms?
2. How many hours did the English students spend at school?
3. Which was the "big night"? Say why.

## B. Language

***Find the following words in the text.***

1. to come back
2. the opposite of outside
3. A place where you can spend your free time.

***Find the correct preposition.***

4. The students had to stay ... school until 5 p.m.
5. They all talked ... the big night.
6. The Germans were interested ... almost everything.

## C. Translation

***Translate the following text into German.***

It was the big night and everybody was very excited. The girls had been invited to go to a disco with some of their new friends. The boys didn't like the idea of going to discos, so they went to the leisure centre instead. There they thought they would have a lot of fun.

## D. Guided writing

### 1. Opinion

*Read the following sentences and say whether you agree or not. Give reasons.*

1. Going to a disco is great fun.
2. German students should also wear school uniforms.

### 2. A Picture Story

*Look at the following pictures and describe what happened to some of the young people who wanted to spend a night at the disco.*

*Write about 80 words. Find a suitable headline and end the story.*

## Northern Ireland

There are miles of untouched countryside and tiny fishing villages along the coast of Northern Ireland.

The people are friendly and helpful. But still there is a lot of trouble in Northern Ireland. Children there quickly learn that it is important which religious group they belong to: either the Catholics or the Protestants.

There is a lot of violence, especially in the bigger cities like, for example, Derry or Belfast. There Catholics and Protestants live in different areas and go to separate schools.

The worst fighting goes on between radical groups: the Catholic I.R.A. and the Protestant U.D.A. The I.R.A. want a united and independent Ireland. They want the British army to leave the country. The U.D.A. is fighting to keep Northern Ireland a part of the United Kingdom.

The British Army was sent to Northern Ireland in 1969 to put an end to violence between Catholics and Protestants. Since the beginning of the troubles there have been many street fights and terrorist attacks in which a lot of people have been killed.

### A. Comprehension

***Read the text and answer the questions in complete sentences.***

1. What is the countryside of Northern Ireland like?
2. What is the difference between the U.D.A. and the I.R.A.?
3. Has the British army succeeded in stopping the violence?

## B. Comprehension

*Find the following words in the text*

1. very small
2. not the same
3. a synonym for particular(ly)

**Adjective or adverb?**

4. The countryside of Northern Ireland is (quiet) ...
5. But in the cities some terrorists act (violent) ...
6. Irish people are (friendly) ...
7. They treat you (friendly) ...

## C. Translation

*Translate the following text into German.*

Some places in Northern Ireland have changed because of all the trouble. Houses have been damaged, shops had to close down and therefore many people have moved away. Protestants and Catholics live in two different areas in the town.

## D. Guided writing

### 1. Asking questions

***Mrs Brown, a tourist from the USA asks Debbie, an Irish girl, about the troubles in Northern Ireland. Ask Mrs Brown's questions.***

*Mrs Brown:* ... ?
*Debbie:* I'm a Protestant.
*Mrs Brown:* ... ?
*Debbie:* No, there are no Catholics at our school.
*Mrs Brown:* ... ?
*Debbie:* No, all my friends are Protestants.
*Mrs Brown:* ... ?
*Debbie:* No, I have never been to the USA.

### 2. A report

***There has been a terrorist attack in Portadown, a town in Northern Ireland. Write a report about it. Write about 80 words.***

| | |
|---|---|
| **Place:** | Portadown |
| **Time:** | Saturday, 8.20 p.m. |
| **Persons:** | three I.R.A. terrorists |
| **Action:** | terrorists - jeep - stopped in front of supermarket - bomb - shop damaged - no people hurt - British army soldiers - follow jeep - jeep too fast - terrorists escaped |

# THE IRISH TROUBLES - HISTORICAL ROOTS

The "troubles" in Ireland, as they are called, have a very long history. The Reformation in the sixteenth century made England a Protestant country. Ireland, however, did not accept this and remained Catholic. This was dangerous for England, as France and Spain were powerful Catholic enemies and might try to use Ireland as a base from which to attack England. English kings and queens therefore tried to get Ireland under their control and force the Irish to become Protestants. Irish lands were taken from the Irish and given to English and Scottish Protestants, especially in the north of the country where Catholics were strong. The Catholic Irish had to pay high rents to these Protestant landowners.

By the nineteenth century, of course, these Protestants were just as Irish as the Catholics. But they were still the people with the money, the people who ruled the country. The Catholic Irish stayed poor.

Many died of starvation, or left the country for America. So the conflict between Protestants and Catholics in Ireland has its roots in the conflict between an upper class and a lower class, between the rich and the poor.

## A. Comprehension

***Answer the following questions in complete sentences.***

1. Why did the British think it was dangerous that Ireland remained Catholic?
2. What did English queens and kings do to bring Ireland under their control?
3. What happened to the Catholics in Ireland?

## B. Language

***Find the word in the text for***

1. one hundred years
2. to die of hunger

***Write down the opposite of the words in bold print.***

3. Many of them stayed **poor.**
4. France and Spain were **powerful** enemies.
5. Land was **given to** the Protestants.

***Write a complete sentence to explain the meaning of the following words.***

6. dangerous
7. conflict

## C. Translation

***Translate the following text into German.***

During the last century many people from Ireland were very poor. There was not enough food to feed all the people. Therefore about one million people left the country and emigrated to America. A lot of Irish people who stayed in Ireland died of starvation.

## D. Guided writing

### 1. Opinion

***Say whether you agree or disagree.***
***Give reasons.***

1. Belfast is a good place for holidays.
2. The Irish countryside is beautiful.

### 2. Letter writing

***You want to spend your holidays in Ireland.***
***Write a letter to***

Mrs Williams
The Mansion
33 Shannon Street
Carrick-on-Shannon

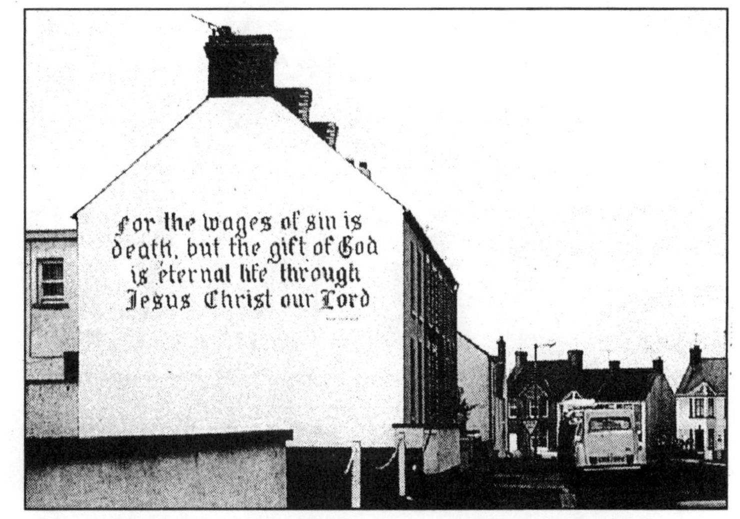


**Sign of the times: an alternative message for Dungannon**

***Tell her that you want to stay at her house with your family, give exact dates, say how many persons will stay, ask about the price.***

***Write about 80 words.***

## THE TWO IRELANDS

The poverty and suffering of the Irish Catholic population in the last century led to demands for independence from Britain. By 1914 the British government was ready to agree to this. But the Irish Protestants refused to accept the idea. The only solution was to divide the country into a Protestant Northern Ireland and a Catholic Southern Ireland. Northern Ireland stayed in the UK, but with its own government. Southern Ireland later became a completely independent country, the Republic of Ireland.

But this has not solved the problems in Northern Ireland, where there is also a large Catholic population which suffered from Protestant discrimination right up to the late 1960s. This led to violent conflict in 1969, which has lasted ever since, with British troops trying to keep the peace between the two sides.

Britain has introduced equal rights for Protestants and Catholics, but many Catholics, after years of discrimination against them, want to see Northern Ireland become part of the Republic.

Britain will not allow this, as most of the population are Protestants and want to remain separate from the Republic. This is what makes the situation so difficult to solve. Meanwhile the violence continues.

### A. Comprehension

*Answer the following questions in complete sentences.*

1. What did the British government agree to in 1914?
2. Why haven't the problems been solved in Northern Ireland?
3. Why won't Britain allow Northern Ireland to become a part of the Republic?

## B. Language

*Find the corresponding noun.*

1. poor
2. to solve
3. to discriminate

*Find the opposites for*

4. next
5. to accept
6. small

## C. Translation

*Translate the following text into German.*

Still today there are problems in Ireland. The British troops are trying to keep the peace between the two sides, but this is not easy to do. The Catholics want to see Northern Ireland become part of the Republic.

## D. Guided writing

### 1. Interpreting

***Herr Schmidt is staying in Ireland with his family. He is talking to Mr Johnson, but he doesn't speak English. His son Peter has to interprete. You are Peter now.***

| | |
|---|---|
| *Herr Schmidt:* | Wie heißen sie? |
| *Peter:* | ... ? |
| *Mr Johnson:* | My name is Johnson. |
| *Herr Schmidt:* | Ich heiße Schmidt. |
| *Peter:* | ... . |
| *Mr Johnson:* | Do you like Ireland? |
| *Peter:* | ... ? |
| *Herr Schmidt:* | Ja, die Landschaft ist sehr schön und einsam. |
| *Peter:* | ... . |
| *Mr Johnson:* | How long are you going to stay in Ireland? |
| *Peter:* | ... ? |
| *Herr Schmidt:* | Drei Wochen. |
| *Peter:* | ... . |
| *Mr Johnson:* | Enjoy your holiday with us. |
| *Peter:* | ... . |

### 2. Summary

***Write a short text about the situation of***

a) Northern Ireland
b) the Republic of Ireland

***today.***

***Don't copy complete sentences from the text. Write about 80 words.***

## THE CONTINUING PROBLEMS OF NORTHERN IRELAND

Northern Ireland could be such a beautiful part of the United Kingdom. With its green hills and lovely beaches it seems to be a peaceful place. But is it really?

The Irish had been leading simple lives for many centuries. They were proud to be the religious centre of Europe. All over the country you can still visit the ruins of once famous Catholic churches and monasteries. But this peaceful life came to a sudden end in 1603. Now the Protestant King James I controlled the country and gave most of the land to Protestant settlers from England and Scotland. The Irish had no more rights in their own country.

In 1846 and the following years the potato crop was very bad. Most potatoes could not be eaten, they were black inside. But still the Irish had to send the good potatoes to England and most people had no money to buy bread. So hundreds of thousands of poor Catholic Irishmen died of hunger. Over a million Irish emigrated to America.

### A. Comprehension

***Read the text and answer the questions in complete sentences.***

1. Which parts of the countryside are so lovely in Ireland?
2. Until which year was Ireland a Catholic country?
3. When did poor Catholics die by the thousands?

### B. Language

***Write a complete sentence to explain the meaning of the following words.***

1. a ruin of a church
2. a settler
3. to emigrate

***Use the words in brackets to make new words and write them down.***

4. (settlers) A lot of red-haired Scots ... in Ireland.
5. (life) The red-haired people who ... in Ireland today had Scottish forefathers.
6. (proud) The starving Irish lost their ... and accepted the dirtiest jobs for very little money.

**Tenses**

***Write down the correct verb form.***

7. (to be) Tourists who visit the Republic of Ireland today ... safe.
8. (to explode) But terrorists ... another bomb in Enniskillen last week,
9. (to hide) the bomb ... in a car.
10. (to kill / to injure) So six people ... and two more ...

### C. Translation

***Translate the following text into German.***

Most Irish had been living in primitive huts for many centuries. Even today you can see large numbers of the simple one-room houses. Sometimes you can smell the smoke coming from their open fires. Then you know that people still live there.

## D. Letter writing

***Write a letter of about 80 words. Describe what you saw on a trip to Ireland.***

Write about
- the countryside
- ruins
- red-haired people
- simple huts

## IRELAND IN THE TWENTIETH CENTURY

The Catholic Irish had fought for independence throughout the centuries, but the worst fighting began in the streets of Dublin on Easter Monday in 1916. The Easter Rising failed, but the violence continued.

Finally Britain divided Ireland into two parts in 1921. Northern Ireland with its majority of Protestants stayed under British rule. The southern part of Ireland became independent. First it called itself the Irish Free State, but after 1949 it became the Republic of Ireland.

As the Protestants still had more power and better jobs in Northern Ireland, the Catholics there wanted to be part of the Republic, too.

Since 1969, more and more British soldiers have been sent to Northern Ireland to keep the peace. But they have not been able to stop the terrorists. A lot of lives have been lost on both sides. Bombs and guns have been killing people almost every week up to today. And nobody can say when it will all stop.

### A. Comprehension

***Read the text and answer the questions in complete sentences.***

1. Why were there more conflicts after Easter Monday 1916?
2. When did the Catholic part of Ireland get its independence?
3. What makes the Catholics so angry in Northern Ireland?

### B. Language

***Write down the words in the text for***

1. most awful
2. the largest number of votes or people
3. the opposite of war

***Use the words in brackets to make new words and write them down.***

4. (independence) The Catholics in Northern Ireland want to be ...
5. (divide) A ... of Northern Ireland is impossible.
6. (violence) Fighting in the streets of Londonderry has been very ...
7. (power) My moped is faster than yours because it is more ...
8. (lives) I liked the ... show on television last night.

***Write down the adjective or adverb needed to complete the following sentences.***

9. (bad) The smoke coming from Irish peat fires smells ...
10. (easier) Today you can find a hamburger restaurant ... than a fish and chips shop.

## C. Translation

***Translate the following text into German.***

The British soldiers cannot stop the terrorists. Every week you can read reports that bombs have been killing people. And nobody can say when it will all stop.

## D. Guided writing

**What do you think?**

***Say whether you agree or disagree with the following statements and why.***
***Choose only two of the following statements.***

1. The British should give Northern Ireland back to the Irish.
2. The Protestants, who have lived in Northern Ireland for centuries, have a right to stay.
3. There should be a fair election in Northern Ireland about the country's future.
4. If Great Britain withdraws from Northern Ireland more people will lose their lives.

**Province divided: a British soldier patrols a Belfast street as fears grow of renewed violence. Some 3,000 people have died in the 'troubles'**

# A NEWS REPORT

A man has been killed and another seriously wounded by British troops in Northern Ireland. The event occurred late this afternoon at an army checkpoint in South Armagh. The two men, who were known to be members of the illegal I.R.A., were travelling in their Ford Escort towards Newry when they were stopped by troops shortly after 4.30 pm. Soldiers found nothing in the car, and therefore allowed it to continue on its way. However, there was another road-block just two hundred yards away from the first one. This time the vehicle did not stop on request, but simply drove straight on, knocking down and injuring a soldier standing in the road. As the car tried to escape, other soldiers opened fire, killing the driver and shooting his passenger in the left arm and right shoulder.

Neither of the men in the car was armed, and the car itself contained no guns or explosives. The Northern Irish police are now examining what happened closely. There are two questions the police are asking: Firstly, why did the car not stop at the second checkpoint? Secondly, why did the soldiers not just shoot at the wheels of the car? This would have been possible. Was it really necessary to shoot to kill?

## A. Comprehension

***Answer the following questions in complete sentences.***

1. Why did the soldiers allow the car to continue on its way?
2. Why did the soldiers shoot at the car?
3. What questions are the Northern Irish police examining?

## B. Language

***Find the words in the text for***

1. hurt
2. the opposite of legal
3. cars and buses

***Explain the meaning of the following words in complete sentences.***

4. a road-block
5. a passenger

***Use the words in brackets to make new words and write them down.***

6. (to kill) Mr McKnife is a dangerous ...
7. (to examine) Next year we'll have to take our ...

## C. Translation

***Translate the following text into German.***

Once again two people were seriously injured by British soldiers when a car didn't stop at an army checkpoint. Two dangerously looking terrorists took their guns and tried to kill the soldiers. Two policemen who were watching the incident from behind a tree opened the fire with their submachine guns.

## D. Guided writing

### 1. Asking questions

***Du bist in Irland zu Besuch und hast die Gelegenheit, mit einem britischen Soldaten zu sprechen. Frage ihn folgendes:***

1. wie lange er schon in Irland ist
2. ob seine Arbeit sehr gefährlich ist
3. ob er manchmal Angst vor Terroristen hat
4. wann er wieder zurück nach England darf

### 2. A picture story

***Write a story about the follwing pictures. Write about 80 words.***

## FIRST JOB

O'Rourke drove the car fast through the dark Derry countryside, laughing now and then at the jokes Flanagan was telling.
"What's the difference between a Brit and a donkey?"
"No idea," answered O'Rourke. "There isn't one," said Flanagan, "but don't tell your donkey, or he might kick you." The driver roared with laughter.

In the back Billy sat rigidly, his face pale and without expression. Why had he got involved in all this? It was the first time. And as he thought of the guns and explosives in the car trunk, he swore that it would be the last.

"Don't you like my jokes, then, Billy?" said Flanagan, turning round to the boy.
"Leave him alone," said O'Rourke. "It's his first job. He's nervous."
"Nervous! Why?" Flanagan laughed. "No soldiers out here, you know. They're all in bed, the bastards." He laughed. "You're going to enjoy working with us, Billy. Friendly team, flexible working hours, plenty of further training, opportunity to become well-known." He laughed again, more loudly.

Billy stared at the road ahead, praying silently that they would meet no army patrol. Survival was all he wanted now, survival and a warm bed.

### A. Comprehension

***Read the text and answer the questions in complete sentences.***

1. Why was Billy so pale?
2. What were the three men about to do?
3. Why did Billy hope that there was no army patrol?

### B. Language

***Write a complete sentence to explain the meaning of the following words.***

1. a joke
2. to stare

***Write down the words in the text for***

3. to have a silent dialogue with God
4. to have very white skin without blood in it

***Use the words in brackets to make new words and write them down.***

5. (survival) Billy hoped that he would .... the night.
6. (to laugh) The air was full of ... .
7. (to tell) Little Red Riding Hood is a well-known fairy ... .

**Tenses**

***Write down the correct verb forms.***

8. (to be) Billy ... never ... on a trip like that before.
9. (not / to like) Billy ... Flanagan's jokes last night.

***Write down the adjective or adverb needed to complete the following sentences.***

10. (quiet) Billy sat there very ... .
11. (dangerous) Driving explosives around can be very ... .

## C. Translation

***Translate the following text into German.***

O'Rourke drove the car fast through the dark Derry countryside, laughing now and then at the jokes Flanagan was telling. In the back Billy sat rigidly, his face pale and without expression. Why had he got involved in all this? It was the first time.

## D. Guided writing

### 1. What do you say?

***You have just seen an accident on a country road. While others are helping the injured people, you are telephoning the police.***

This is what you have to report:

a) name: say your name
b) where: accident near Half-Way-Inn outside Sheerness
c) what: two cars, a crash
d) who: two or three people injured

### 2. What do you think?

***Say whether you agree or disagree with the following statements and why.***
***Choose only two of the following statements.***

a) The British should leave at once.
b) There should be a democratic election first before the British leave.
c) Without the British soldiers there would be more trouble.
d) Billy can't wait to kill a British soldier.

## FROM COMMONWEALTH TO EEC

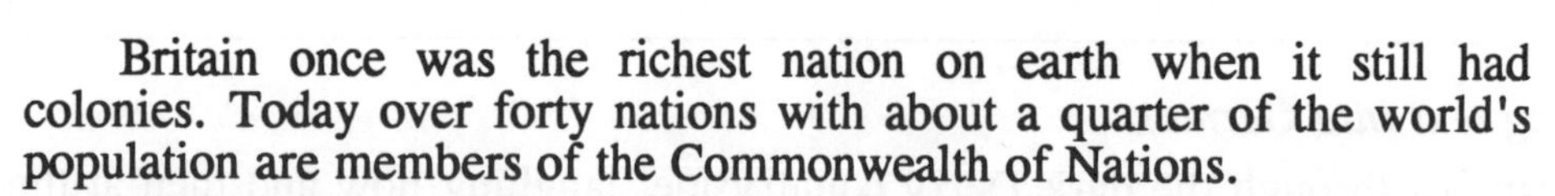

Britain once was the richest nation on earth when it still had colonies. Today over forty nations with about a quarter of the world's population are members of the Commonwealth of Nations.

When the colonies became independent they decided to trade with the other Commonwealth countries. There are meetings between businessmen, politicians and artists. Sometimes there are problems because of all the different people and races and customs. This, however, is not very surprising if you think how different they are. Just think of the Canadians and the Indians.

Many people from the states of the Commonwealth have moved to Britain so today there is a large group of non-white immigrants.

Then Britain looked for trading partners and decided to join the EEC, the European Economic Community. Many British were against this membership at first but now British industry has realized that this market is a chance to export its products to the continent.

### A. Comprehension

***Read the text and answer the questions in complete sentences.***

1. When was Britain the richest nation on earth?
2. Why are there problems sometimes?
3. Why did Britain join the EEC?

### B. Language

***Find the words in the text for***

1. 25%
2. people who go to another country to live there

***Explain the following words in complete sentences.***

3. population
4. products

***Put the following verbs into their correct tenses.***

5. (to have) Britain ... colonies all over the world before World War I.
6. (to trade) Today the British ... with their partners of the EEC.
7. (to show) Future ... if Britain's membership with the EEC will turn out to be a success.

### C. Translation

***Translate the following text into German.***

After British colonies had become independent the nation had to look for new trading partners. Finally the British government decided to join the EEC. Many people were against this membership at first, but now more and more people realize that the common market is a good chance to export British products to the continent.

## D. Guided writing

### 1. Opinion

*Say whether you agree or not. Give reasons.*

1. Non-white immigrants should not be allowed to live in Britain.
2. The EEC is a good chance for European countries.

### 2. Letter writing

*Shashikala, an Indian girl, had come to London to live there. Everything seems strange to her. She writes a letter home in English. She writes about*

- where she lives now
- the weather in England
- food
- lots of people in the streets
- her new job

*Write Shashikala's letter. Write about 80 words.*

**The original countries in 1957:**
Belgium
Federal Republic of Germany
France
Italy
Luxemburg
The Netherlands

**More members joined in 1973:**
Denmark
Great Britain
Ireland

**in 1981:**
Greece

**in 1986:**
Portugal
Spain

# IMMIGRANTS IN GREAT BRITAIN

Great Britain no longer is an Empire with colonies all over the world. But millions of people came from the former colonies to live in Britain. Most of these new British live in the industrial towns where they try to live close to other people who originally came from the same countries.

So you can see Indian or Pakistani neighbourhoods, for example, complete with little shops and restaurants offering clothes or food from their distant home countries. Indian families are especially keen on giving their children the best possible school education. They expect a lot of their children and encourage them to take up careers as doctors, laywers or computer scientists. A recent survey found that Indian and South-East Asian pupils did far better at school than children coming from white working-class parents. That is why an eleven year-old boy named Ganesh Sittapalam could begin studying for a mathematics degree at Surrey University in 1991.

Unfortunately, there are white radicals who don't like all this. They organized "Rights for Whites" marches which ended in bloody fights between Indians and English people. The young Indians hope the police will protect them better in the future.

## A. Comprehension

***Read the text and answer the questions in complete sentences.***

1. Where did the immigrants in Great Britain mostly come from?
2. Why are many Indian children better pupils?
3. Where do a lot of Indians live in Great Britain?

## B. Language

***Write down the words in the text for***

1. A third world country belonging to a white western country.
2. A person who can advise people about the law.

***Replace the verbs in bold print by words or expressions which mean more or less the same.***

3. A **student** goes to school to learn a lot of things.
4. You must be nice to your **father and mother.**

***Connect the following sentences by using one of these conjunctions:***
***when, as long as, although, because***

5. Ganesh was accepted at University. He was only 11 years old.
6. He can go to University. He has an A-level in maths.
7. His parents were very happy. They found out that he was extremely intelligent.

***Use the words in brackets to make new words and write them down.***

8. (to live) Ganesh's ... is quite different from his friends' ....

**Tenses**

***Write down the correct verb forms.***

9. (to have) Great Britain ... a lot of colonies.
10. (to feel) Indians usually ... safer when they live in Indian neighbourhoods.

## C. Translation

***Translate the following text into German.***

Indian fathers expect a lot of their children. They support them as much as possible so they can become doctors or lawyers. So Indian and South-East Asia pupils often get better marks at school than children coming from white working-class parents.

## D. Guided writing

### 1. What do you think?

***Say whether you agree or disagree with the following statements and why.***
***Choose only two of the following statements.***

1. White pupils could be better if their parents were more interested in their school work.
2. Indian pupils are cleverer than English pupils.
3. Indian laywers are better than English lawyers.
4. As an Indian I would prefer to go to an Indian doctor.

### 2. Interpreting

***On a trip to England you have to help a German tourist who doesn't speak any English. He is ill and needs a doctor's attention.***

| | |
|---|---|
| *Doctor:* | Good morning. What can I do for you? You seem to have a temperature. |
| *You:* | ... |
| *Tourist:* | Ich fühle mich nicht wohl. Es begann, nachdem ich gestern abend in einem Hamburger-Restaurant gegessen hatte. |
| *You:* | ... |
| *Doctor:* | Did you eat hamburgers or anything with chicken? |
| *You:* | ... |
| *Tourist:* | Ja, sage ihm, daß ich Hamburger und Hühnchen gegessen habe. |
| *You:* | ... |
| *Doctor:* | It looks like food poisoning. Take these tablets with water and you will feel better tomorrow. |
| *You:* | ... |

## ENGLISH - A WORLD LANGUAGE

English is the mother tongue of more than 350 million people in the world. Among these are Britain, the USA, Canada, Australia, New Zealand and South Africa. For a further 300 million it is an official second language.

Many countries in Africa and Asia which used to be British colonies have more than one native language. India, for example, has fifteen main languages, besides a large number of less important ones. So it is not surprising that English has been kept as a common language. Without it a lot of Indians would not be able to talk to one another! Since the last war the use of English as a worldwide language has spread far beyond the British Commonwealth.

America's position as a world power has led to a worldwide use of English in many areas. Trade, politics, sport, and engineering are just a few of them. Wherever international experts meet, talk, speak or write, they express their ideas in English.

### A. Comprehension

***Read the text and answer the questions in complete sentences.***

1. Why is English still an important language in India?
2. Since when has English become the most important language of international communication?
3. Do most of those who speak English speak it as their mother tongue?

### B. Language

***Write a complete sentence to explain the meaning of the following words.***

1. mother tongue
2. native language
3. experts

***Write down the adjective or adverb needed to complete the following sentences.***

4. (easy) You can learn English more ... than Chinese.
5. (good) Indian food tastes ... .
6. (correct) Even if you can't speak English ... you can make yourself understood.

**If-clauses**

***Complete the following sentences and write down the correct verb form.***

7. (to understand) If you travel to former British colonies almost everybody ... you.
8. (to learn) If I ... more English words, I would have been able to understand that book.

### C. Translation

***Translate the following text into German.***

Trade, politics, sport, and engineering are just a few of the areas where English is used in almost every country. International experts usually express their ideas in English in magazines and at conferences.

## D. Guided writing

**What do you think?**

***Say whether you agree or disagree with the following statements and why. Choose only two of the following statements.***

1. You can't become a famous sportsman if you don't speak English.
2. English is more important than German when you work with computers.
3. English is very helpful when you go on holiday.
4. Every pupil should go to England or America for a year to learn English perfectly.

## ACCENTS

A few years ago all you heard on radio and television was "Oxford English", the accent of the old upper class. It is called "Oxford English" because of Oxford University, where the aristocracy was educated. In order to be accepted anywhere in public life, whether as a politician, or a television star, or even as a schoolteacher, you had to speak "Oxford English". Up to the 1960s no Prime Minister ever spoke anything but Oxford English, and the Royal Family still speak it even today.

But things have changed. The power of the upper class has almost disappeared. As a result, today's "Standard English" is the kind of English spoken by any ordinary educated person of any class in London and the South of England.

Nowadays, though, no one is forced even to speak Standard English. Regional accents are not only accepted, but encouraged, even on radio and television. Television itself has made everyone used to hearing Birmingham, Liverpool or Newcastle English, or the accents of Scotland, Wales and Ireland. Everyone understands them, and a lot of people in the South like listening to them.

### A. Comprehension

***Read the text and answer the questions in complete sentences.***

1. Where did the name "Oxford English" come from?
2. Who spoke Oxford English until a few years ago?
3. Why did most people try to speak Oxford English?
4. Why don't even BBC announcers speak Oxford English any more?

### B. Language

***Replace the verbs in bold print by words or expressions which mean more or less the same.***

1. The Queen and her family are among the **richest** people in Great Britain.
2. The use of Oxford English has almost completely **gone away** in radio and television.

***Write a complete sentence to explain the meaning of the following words.***

3. accent
4. ordinary person

***Write down the words in the text for***

5. the title of the man or woman who is the political leader of Great Britain.
6. in our time

***Add the correct preposition and write the full expression.***

7. Can I speak ... your brother?
8. I have been looking everywhere ... him.
9. I had no time to come round because I had to take care ... my little brother.
10. Perhaps we can go ... the cinema together.

## C. Translation

***Translate the following text into German.***
A few years ago all you heard on radio and television was "Oxford English". Every politician or schoolteacher who wanted to be accepted in public life had to speak "Oxford English". Up to the 1960s no Prime Minister ever spoke anything but Oxford English.

## D. Guided writing

**What do you think?**

***Say whether you agree or disagree with the following statements and why.***
***Choose only two of the following statements.***

1. Having a standard language like Oxford English is better for international communication than a number of regional accents.
2. Everybody should be able to speak the standard language fluently.
3. It is perfectly all right if you can hear from which class or region a speaker comes.
4. People who speak with an accent are thought to be less intelligent than accent-free speakers.

## A THIEF OF A LANGUAGE

English, with over 400,000 words, is a very rich language. But many of these words have been stolen from other languages. In the following story there are seven such words:

When old Mrs Mills came to the zebra crossing, she put down her shopping bag and waited. The thief, who was standing behind the telephone kiosk, saw his chance. He ran to the crossing and quickly picked up the bag. But old Mrs Mills was even quicker. She took her umbrella and hit the thief with it over the head. He dropped the bag and ran away.

"Stop the man in the red anorak!" shouted Mrs Mills. Then she went down on her knees and picked up ten tomatoes, six hamburgers and a small bottle of vodka. "I need a drop of that!" said old Mrs Mills.

**The words and their origins are:**

"zebra" ▶ Bantu
"kiosk" ▶ Persian
"umbrella" ▶ Italian
"anorak" ▶ Inuit
"tomato" ▶ Nahuatl
"hamburger" ▶ German
"vodka" ▶ Russian

### A. Comprehension

*Read the text and answer the questions in complete sentences.*

1. Why has English got so many words?
2. Why did Mrs Mills put down her shopping bag?
3. Why did the thief drop the bag again?

### B. Language

*Write down the words in the text for*

1. taking something away without paying for it.
2. a piece of clothing which you wear in the rain.
3. the part of the street where you can get to the other side of the street.

*Complete the sentences by using the opposites of the words in brackets.*

4. (rich) Poland is a ... country.
5. (to pick up) The planes ... boxes of food.
6. (small) Next time Mrs Mills is going to buy a ... bottle of vodka.

*Write down the correct verb form.*

7. (to arrest) The thief ... by the police last night.
8. (to appear) The thief ... in court tomorrow.
9. (to send) Perhaps he ... to prison by the judge for some weeks then.
10. (not / to improve) If the thief's attitudes ... the police will watch him carefully.

## C. Translation

***Translate the following text into German.***

English has got over 400,000 words. But many of these words have been taken from other languages. Not only did the colonialists bring home words for food such as maize or tomato from America, they also learned new words in India. There they found words like veranda or bungalow. These words were then handed on to German, too.

## D. Guided writing

**Writing a report**

***Write a report of about 100 words about foreign words in German. Do you think there are too many of those words?***

***Think of these words:***

- Kaiser (from caesar, Latin)
- Pforte, Portal (from porta = door, Latin)
- Chauffeur (from chauffer = to heat, French)
- Friseur (from friser = hairdresser, French)
- Coiffeur (from coiffure = hairdresser, French)
- fair play (English)
- Video-Cassette (English)

## JOBS THEN AND NOW

Some centuries ago there weren't many jobs to choose from. Most people were farmers or labourers, if they lived in the country. Others were bakers or butchers. Today things are different; there are hundreds of different kinds of jobs. Many of these require special skills of one kind or another.

If you think choosing a job is not easy you are right. But there are people who will help you in your effort to find a proper job. There is the careers teacher you can talk to at school. Or you can also go the the local careers officer. He can advise about which jobs are available at the moment.

Don't forget to ask yourself what kind of work you would like to do before deciding. Do you like talking to people? Do you want to help people? Do you like working with computers? The answers to questions like these might help you decide.

If you have found a job you will realize that many firms today work with computers. High technology has killed off some jobs but also created new ones. So be ready to work with these machines because more and more jobs require knowledge and skill in the use of computers.

### A. Comprehension

***Answer the following questions in complete sentences.***

1. Why is it not easy to find a job today?
2. Who will help you to find a proper job?
3. In what way can you help yourself?

### B. Language

***Find the words in the text for***

1. 100 years
2. ability
3. to find out

*Complete the following sentences by using each of these conjunctions only once: because - if - although*

4. He asked the careers teacher ... he could help him to find a job.
5. He wanted to become a baker ... he didn't want to get up early.
6. Susan wanted to become a travel agent ... she likes talking to people.

## C. Translation

***Translate the following text into German.***

Today there are over two hundred different jobs to choose from. Therefore it would be a good idea to contact the careers teacher or your local careers officer before choosing a job. Above all you should also ask yourself what kind of work you would like to do most.

## D. Guided writing

### 1. Conversation

***Peter wants to become a computer expert. He is sitting at the careers officer's office who is asking him questions.***

*Officer:* ... ?
*Peter:* I'm seventeen.
*Officer:* ... ?
*Peter:* Yes, I have already worked for a big firm in my holidays.
*Officer:* ... ?
*Peter:* No, I don't mind working at weekends.
*Officer:* ... ?
*Peter:* Yes, I like talking to people.

### 2. Letter writing

**House sitter wanted.**

Young man or lady who wants to spend 4 weeks in California who has to take care of our house while we are on holiday. Huge garden, swimming pool, car available.

Apply to
George Smith
10324 El Paso Ave.
Los Angeles Ca 92189

***Write a letter of application and say who you are and why you would like to do the job. Write about 80 words.***

## A DREAM JOB FOR SAMANTHA

Samantha Benson has just left Salisbury Comprehensive School. She has finished school with good examination results in five subjects. And with five GCSEs (General Certificates of Secondary Education) she has very good chances of getting a good job. So she looked at all the adverts in the local paper and even went to the local job centre for advice. She answered a number of interesting adverts. One of them offered training as a sales person in a pet shop, another training as a veterinary nurse and a third offered a job at the local zoo.

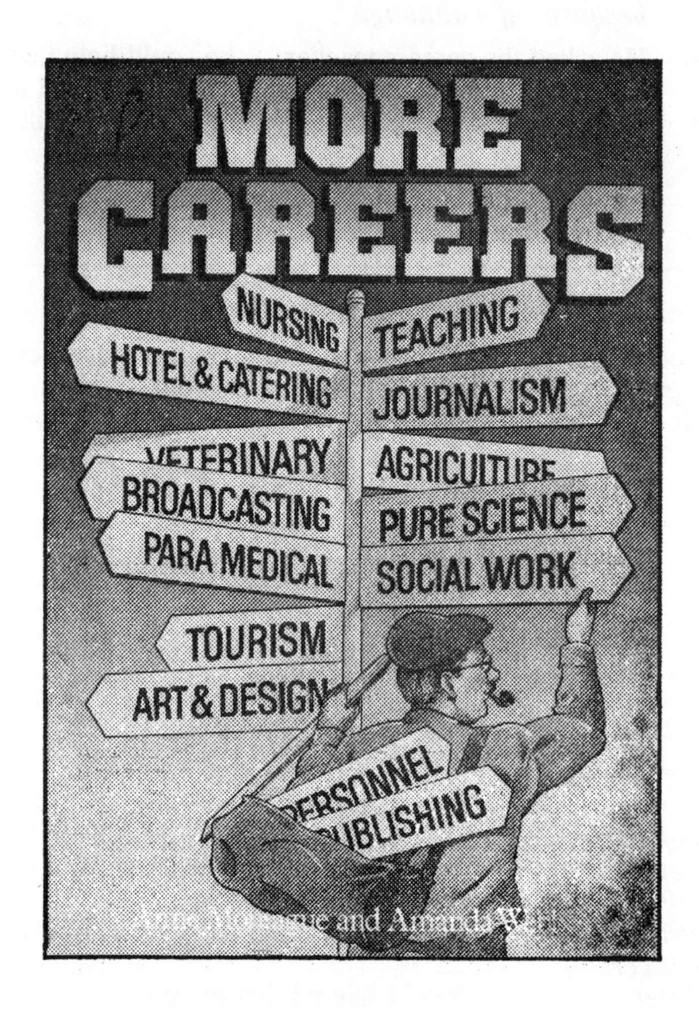


Her mother was against all of these jobs. She was sure the pay would be bad and she would have to work in the evenings, too, and even at the weekends if she took the job at the zoo. Her mother wanted her to look for a nice nine-to-five job in an office. There Samantha could use her good exam results in English and perhaps French, but never as a zoo keeper or a vet's assistant.

### A. Comprehension

***Read the text and answer the questions in complete sentences.***

1. What sort of job is Samantha most interested in?
2. Why should Samantha be able to find an excellent job?
3. Why didn't Samantha's mother like Samantha's dream jobs?

### B. Language

***Write down the words in the text for***

1. a doctor for animals.
2. a person who sells things in shops.

***Use the words in brackets to make new words and write them down.***

3. (examination) Samantha was ... in five subjects.
4. (education) Teachers and parents try to ... boys and girls.
5. (advertisement) In the Saturday paper hundreds of jobs are ... .

***Add the correct preposition and write the full expression.***

6. Samantha asked ... Sally's telephone number.
7. Sally has no chance ... finding a job.
8. Sally is keen ... becoming an actress.

## C. Translation

***Translate the following text into German.***

Samantha's mother wanted her to look for a nice office job with regular hours. There the pay would be better and Samantha could use her good exam results in English and French.

## D. Guided writing

**Asking questions**

***You have applied for a job. In this interview you are talking to your new boss.***

*Boss:* Have you got any more questions about this job?
*You:* (to pay - how much - per week?)
*Boss:* You'll get a starting salary of £25.
*You:* (holidays - how many days - per year?)
*Boss:* In the first year you'll get two days for every month that you have worked for us.
*You:* (to work - in the evenings?)
*Boss:* Not, not very often.
*You:* (to say - more exactly?)
*Boss:* Well, perhaps two or three times every month.
*You:* (normal working hours?)
*Boss:* In the morning we begin at a quarter to nine. There is a lunch break of one hour and work ends at half past five.
*You:* (work - on Saturdays?)
*Boss:* No, the office is closed on Saturdays.

## A LETTER FOR SAMANTHA

Sam, as Samantha was usually called by her friends, didn't want to listen to her mother's advice. She wanted to work with animals and not in an office.

On Friday morning the first letter arrived in answer to her applications. It was from the vet. It read:

> Dear Mr Benson,
>
> Thank you for your application as a veterinary nurse. Although I have never heard of a young man working as a veterinary nurse I'll give you a chance. Sometimes we have to operate on heavy dogs, so a strong assistant could be very useful from time to time.
>
> I would be pleased to give you an interview at 3 p.m. on Monday, September 13th. Please bring your GCSE results and some references.
>
> Yours sincerely,
>
> *J. Greenwald, B.Vet.Med.*

First Sam and Mrs Benson didn't know what to make of the letter. Then Mrs Benson started laughing. "How did you sign your application?"
"Well, I signed it 'Sam Benson' as usual," Samantha replied.
"So he must have thought Sam was a boy's name. He'll be surprised to see a pretty girl at the interview. He has written such a friendly letter. I think he'll be a nice boss, too."

### A. Comprehension

***Read the text and answer the questions in complete sentences.***

1. Why wasn't Mrs Benson against the job in the end?
2. What was the vet's misunderstanding?
3. When can the vet use a strong assistant?

### B. Language

***Complete the sentences by using the opposites of the words in brackets.***

1. (first) The ... letter arrived on Friday.
2. (useful) A vet's assistant who can't see blood is ...
3. (started) Mrs Benson ... laughing.
4. (ugly) Samantha is a ... girl.

***Complete the following sentences by using each of the conjunctions only once:***
***when - as long as - although - because***

5. Samantha wants to work as a vet's assistant. She can't earn a lot of money.
6. She wants to work for a vet. She likes animals.

**Tenses**

***Write down the correct verb forms.***

7. (to write) Every year hundreds of girls ... letters to pop singers.
8. (to arrive) The postman ... just ... with a signed postcard from a famous singer.
9. (to pin) Sam ... the postcard to her wall.
10. (to show) Tomorrow Sam ... it to her friends.

## C. Translation

***Translate the following text into German.***

Thank you for your application as a nurse. We'll give you a chance. Please come for an interview on Monday, August 12th, at 8 o'clock. We hope that you are strong enough for the job. Some of our patients are quite heavy, so a strong assistant could be very useful.

## D. Guided writing

**Letter writing**

***Write Samantha's answer to the vet. Here are some ideas to help you. Write about 100 words.***

- thank you for answer
- girl, not boy
- Sam short for Samantha
- quite strong, father owner of body-building studio
- active in sports
- interview on September 13th o.k.
- only two references: teacher and youth group leader. Enough?

## LEAVING SCHOOL

Brian Rickfield is in the 5th form of a Comprehensive School in Manchester. He is taking his GCSE* this summer. Brian hopes to become a junior clerk with one of the big banks in the city centre.

"I was thinking of looking for a job with an insurance company," Brian explains. "Then I talked to Mrs Bentham who is the careers advisor at our school. I realized that I would prefer dealing with customers to sitting in an office the whole time. I like paper work, but I enjoy meeting people as well, you see." Brian is one of nearly fifteen hundred young people who will be leaving school in the Greater Manchester area this summer.

He will try to pass at least five O-levels*. That means he will have to sit five examinations: in maths, English, French, and two other subjects such as geography, history, or science. Then he hopes to apply successfully for a position as a bank clerk. His favourite subject is maths. "I love working with figures," he says. "I'm also interested in computers. Banks these days do so much of their work on computers. So I think I have a good chance of getting the job I want."

* General Certificate of Education
* Ordinary level

### A. Comprehension

***Read the text and answer the questions in complete sentences.***

1. What was Brian's first idea of a good job?
2. Why did he change his mind?
3. In which town does Brian live?

### B. Language

***Add the correct preposition and write the full expression.***

1. Brian is interested ... finding an exciting job.
2. A lot of young people are looking ... a well-paid job.
3. Brian is looking forward ... dealing with nice customers.

***Write down the adjective or adverb needed to complete the following sentences.***

4. (nice) Brian always does his maths homework ...
5. (interesting) His maths teacher explains new problems ...
6. (good) Brian understands maths very ...
7. (easy) I don't think maths is so ... .

***Write down the correct verb form.***

8. (to leave) Next year 1,500 students ... with O-levels.
9. (to pass) Last summer only 1,300 ... the O-level examinations.
10. (to work) Brian ... already ... with computers.
11. (to have) He says, "You ... better chances to get a good job if you can work with a computer."
12. (to be) A computer ... more useful than a typewriter.

## C. Translation

***Translate the following text into German.***

John Miller will try to pass at least five O-levels. That means he will have to take five examinations: in maths, English, French, and two other subjects such as geography, history, or science. Then he hopes to apply successfully for a position as an assistant in a travel agency.

## D. Guided writing

### 1. Asking questions

***Brian has his first job interview. Here are Brian's answers. Can you find the questions?***

1. ... ?
   Yes, I passed GCSE.
2. ... ?
   I passed in five subjects.
3. ... ?
   My favourite subject is maths.
4. ... ?
   Oh yes, I have already worked with computers.
5. ... ?
   Yes, we learned all about computers at school.
6. ... ?
   No, I haven't got a computer, but I often worked with my friend's computer.

### 2. Find a suitable ending.

***Choose two of the following sentences and complete them.***

7. If you hate foreign languages, you shouldn't ...
8. Working as a newspaper reporter can be ...
9. When you are a pilot, you ...
10. When you work at a travel agency, you can ...

### 3. Writing a report

***Please write a report. Write about 100 words and explain, which job you would like to choose. Name the job and say why you would like to choose it!***

These ideas can help you:

hobbies
subjects at school
father's / mother's job
friend's advice
careers officer's advice
tests at job exchange
advertisements in newspaper
report on television
good chances in the future
good pay

## A LETTER TO JUDY

*4 Rye Lane*
*Sevenoaks*

*Thursday, June 29th*

*Dear Judy,*

*I'm sorry I haven't been in touch for such a long time.*
*Since I was made redundant at Ludlow's four months ago I haven't been able to get another job. I'm a bit depressed, to tell you the truth. That's why I haven't felt like going out much or contacting anybody. Up to now I have applied for about 12 or 13 different jobs, all with firms in the export-import business, like Ludlow's. But I haven't had any luck, I'm afraid.*

*I usually go to the job centre three or four times a week, but they never seem to have much. This week they sent me to an export firm in East London which was looking for somebody to deal with export orders to the Far East. But the manager who interviewed me said that I was too young and inexperienced for the position that was vacant. I'm beginning to think that I should look for a completely different type of occupation, or perhaps go on a re-training programme. I wouldn't mind going into electronics - computers, for example. But at the moment I just feel discouraged and disappointed. Write to me soon and cheer me up.*

*Love,*
*Marion*

### A. Comprehension

***Read the text and answer the questions in complete sentences.***

1. What happened to Marion four months ago?
2. Why is Marion so depressed?
3. What sort of job has Marion been trained to do?

### B. Language

***Write down the words in the text for***

1. a talk with an applicant who wants a job.
2. trying to get a job by writing letters to companies.

*Complete the sentences by using the opposites of the words in brackets.*

3. (sad) Marion is very ... . She has found a job again.
4. (nobody) Now she feels like kissing ... .
5. (important) Her old problems have become ... now.

*Use the words in brackets to make new words and write them down.*

6. (busy) A manager is a ...
7. (discouraged) What you need is a little more ...
8. (to apply) She has written 13 ...
9. (employment) Now Marion is ... at the airport.

## C. Translation

*Translate the following text into German.*

Marion usually goes to the job centre three or four times a week, but they never seem to have much. Last week they sent her to an export firm in East London. But the manager who interviewed her said that she was too young and inexperienced for the position that was vacant.

## D. Guided writing

### 1. Dialogue

*At the job centre. Find the suitable questions to these answers.*

1. ... ?
   My name is Marion Brown.
2. ... ?
   I'm 19.
3. ... ?
   I was made redundant because Ludlow's closed down.
4. ... ?
   I worked in the office.
5. ... ?
   Of course I can type.
6. ... ?
   Yes, I worked with a computer.
7. ... ?
   Certainly I would like to work for a doctor.
8. ... ?
   Yes, I can start tomorrow. How wonderful.

### 2. Letter writing

*Imagine you are Marion. You found a new job as a doctor's secretary and receptionist. (Look at the dialogue above!) Write a letter to your friend Judy. Tell her in about 80 words*

- how you got the job
- how you like the job
- what sort of things you have to do there
- how you like the doctor and the other assistants

# Vocabulary

**S.2**

| | |
|---|---|
| birth | Geburt |
| jail | Gefängnis |
| to claim | beanspruchen |

**S.4**

| | |
|---|---|
| to faint | ohnmächtig werden |
| two-way radio | Funkgerät |
| treatment | Behandlung |

**S.6**

| | |
|---|---|
| to perform | spielen, auftreten |
| games teacher | Sportlehrer |

**S.8**

| | |
|---|---|
| homely | einfach |
| divorced | geschieden |
| secret | Geheimnis |

**S.10**

| | |
|---|---|
| exchange | Austausch |
| to be homesick | Heimweh haben |
| curious | neugierig |
| to wave | winken |

**S.12**

| | |
|---|---|
| stay | Aufenthalt |
| leisure | Freizeit |

**S.14**

| | |
|---|---|
| tiny | winzig |
| either | entweder |

**S.16**

| | |
|---|---|
| roots | Wurzeln |
| to remain | bleiben |
| enemy | Feind |
| base | Basis |
| rent | Pacht, Miete |
| to rule | beherrschen |
| starvation | Unterernährung |

**S.18**

| | |
|---|---|
| suffering | Leiden |
| demand | Forderung |
| to refuse | ablehnen |

**S.20**

| | |
|---|---|
| monastery | Kloster |
| crop | Ernte |
| to emigrate | auswandern |

**S.22**

| | |
|---|---|
| throughout | während, durch |
| Easter Rising | Oster-Aufstand |
| to fail | fehlschlagen |
| majority | Mehrheit |

**S.24**

| | |
|---|---|
| event | Ereignis, Vorfall |
| to occur | sich ereignen |
| checkpoint | Kontrollstelle |
| road-block | Straßensperre |
| request | Aufforderung |
| to injure | verletzen |
| neither | keiner |
| armed | bewaffnet |
| to contain | enthalten |
| explosives | Sprengstoffe |

**S.26**

| | |
|---|---|
| donkey | Esel |
| rigid | steif |
| to get involved | sich einlassen |
| trunk | Kofferraum |
| to swear | schwören |
| to pray | beten |
| survival | das Überleben |

**S.28**

| | |
|---|---|
| to trade | Handel treiben |
| artist | Künstler |
| customs | Gebräuche, Gewohnheiten |

**S.30**

| | |
|---|---|
| Empire | Weltmacht |
| originally | ursprünglich |
| distant | weit entfernt |
| to be keen on | versessen sein auf |
| to encourage | ermutigen |
| lawyer | Rechtsanwalt |
| recent | neu, vor kurzem |
| survey | Umfrage |
| degree | (akademischer) Grad, Tite |

**S.32**

| | |
|---|---|
| mother tongue | Muttersprache |
| further | weitere |
| native | eingeboren, einheimisch |
| engineering | Technik, Ingenieurswesen |

**S.34**

| | |
|---|---|
| aristocracy | Aristokratie, Adel |
| in order to | um zu |
| ordinary | gewöhnlich |
| nowadays | heutzutage |
| though | jedoch |

**S.38**

| | |
|---|---|
| labourer | ungelernter (Land-)Arbeit |
| to require | benötigen |
| skills | Fähigkeiten |
| effort | Anstrengung, Bemühung |
| proper | richtig, angemessen |
| local | örtlich |
| to advise | einen Rat geben |
| available | verfügbar |